CW00407632

Super Funny Text Fails, Autocorrect Fails Mishaps On Smartphones

Ashley Sheffer

© Copyright

All rights reserved

This book is targeted towards offering essential details about the subject covered. The publication is being provided with the thought that the publisher is not mandated to render an accounting or other qualified services. If recommendations are needed, professional or legal, a practiced person in the profession ought to be engaged.

In no way is it legal to recreate, duplicate, or transfer any part of this document in either electronic means or printed format. Copying of this publication is strictly prohibited, and its storage is not allowed unless with written authorization from the publisher. All rights reserved.

The information supplied herein is specified to be honest because any liability in regards to inattention or otherwise, by any use or abuse of any directions, processes, or policies confined within is the sole and utter obligation of the recipient reader. Under no circumstances will any form of legal duty or blame be held against the publisher for any reparation, damages, or financial loss because of the information contained herein. The author owns the entire copyrights not maintained by the publisher.

The information stated herein is provided for educational purposes exclusively. The presentation of the data is without contractual agreement or any kind of warranty assurance.

All trademarks inside this book are for clarifying purposes only and are possessed by the owners themselves, not allied with this document.

Disclaimer

All erudition supplied in this book is specified for educational and academic purposes only. The author is not in any way to be responsible for any outcomes that emerge from using this book. Practical efforts have been made to render information that is both precise and effective. Still, the author is not to be held answerable for the accuracy or use/misuse of this information.

Foreword

I will like to thank you for taking the very first step of trusting me and deciding to purchase/read this life-transforming book. Thanks for investing your time and resources on this product.

I can assure you of precise outcomes if you will diligently follow the specific blueprint I lay bare in the information handbook you are currently checking out. It has transformed lives, and I firmly believe it will equally change your own life too.

All the information I provided in this Do It Yourself piece is easy to absorb and practice.

Table of Contents

SECTION ONE

Introduction

If you own a smartphone, there's a likelihood you've screamed that expression at least once. Perhaps you sent a text to your spouse that you "f 'd like the dog" instead of (fed) In any case, Autocorrect was most likely the offender.

While the feature on our mobile gadgets can be a blessing, it's also frequently a curse. It often alters words without rhyme or factor, and if you hit "send" too quickly, it can cause some funny, complicated, or just plain humiliating results. I found that out the problem when I innocently attempted to invite a couple of pals over for an evening of gelato. My iPhone's Autocorrect, however, had another idea and asked them over for a night of "fellatio." And just like that, Autocorrect turned me into a hussy. What would my mom say!

Shortly after the gelato/fellatio event, I started wondering if other individuals out there were having comparable experiences with their smartphones. From my research, it ended up, and there were millions of individuals who were just as annoyed by Autocorrect as I was.

This book is loaded with hundred humorous images, most of which are found for the first time here that emphasize the unintended hilarity that frequently ensues when Autocorrect goes incorrect. These laugh-out-loud amusing examples can be found in section two of this book.

Text Messages - When Words Seem to Fail

Sending out text is more than a familiar pattern. I can keep in mind when I bought my very first pager and then brand-new pagers capable of getting text messages hit the market, shortly after that, you could send out a text to other text capable pagers. It seems that America and other countries had sent out text messages long before it was capable of cellular phones.

There was a time when pagers, a PDA, and cellular phones were different gadgets, and you would find people carrying all three. Before all of this innovation, people would send by mail letters, make phone calla in your home, or a phone booth; remember those? People use to communicate either deal with to face, via a telephone call, or by a letter sent in the mail.

When talking face to face with a person and if you were to hear a requirement, you felt the sense to reach out and provide some guidance or assistance in such away. Our spoken words appear to connect us.

Text messages changed the way we communicate. When mobile phones ended up being smarted, the more youthful and older generation of techies needed to have these gadgets. So much so, texting surpasses, face to phone, e-mail, and face discussions for ages 12-17 years of age. I'm sure that 15 years back, no one would have ever believed, sending out text would exceed talking with somebody face to face. You could be sitting 10 feet far from someone in your cubicle, and they would instead send out instant messages than to stroll over to you and talk.

The Great Disconnect

Texting is impersonal. You do not have to wait for a response; you never see the facial expression of the one you are communicating with.

When our words appear to stop working with our teen ages (and some adults), sending out a text message is comfy and familiar to them.

Texting, a Threat to the English Language?

A number of us have had our days of putting in additional effort to write correct English without the help (and in some cases, inconvenience) of AutoCorrect. Without the intervention of innovation to ruin us those days, we were more rooted, and maybe, even wiser, as far as the English language is concerned.

We have had our days of letter composing, scribbling ideas on welcoming cards, even endlessly written assessments with clear handwriting. However came the technology, and all of that underwent an extreme change.

The culture of texting has taken a toll on us. In this age of the internet and social networking, the quality of what would otherwise be a continual process of enhancement on the English language has instead become a cause of the issue. Particularly, if you are among those with a deep issue for appropriate use of grammar and spellings, then this age has shown to be rather disappointing as far as it concerns the English language.

How would you want someone to wish you on your birthday with an HBD or GBU? They don't make good sense to me, and I would rather not be wanted at all than to have somebody compose to me in such a way. Today, we also have kids who have their names composed in such an unusual style. In some cases, they come with random apostrophes falling in between. Then, some treat your name as a commodity, no capitalization of the very first letter of your name. Even even worse, official letters that are inclined to the chat terminology.

What initially started as Short Text Messaging, which, 'is the act of composing and sending out a short, electronic message in between two or more cellphones, or repaired or portable devices over a phone network,' has today evolved into something extensively bigger, covering so much more than phone networks alone.

The question is, has texting made our lives much easier, or is it messing up whatever we have correctly found out of the English language? True, there is always the great and the bad of whatever. The case being, the bad emerges when we cross the limitations. In this age, invaded by innovation, it would certainly do us great to do a recheck on ourselves, and begin making an effort to go back to utilizing appropriate English language, unless naturally, you are texting in the true sense.

That way, we would also be able to restore the personal touch of humanity, which we have, to a large extent, lost to texting.

A short message service was created in the early 80s as an interaction means for engineers constructing the mobile network. It has acquired worldwide approval given that its integration into the GSM services, Portio Research 2008, reports that SMS traffic is anticipated to grow across international markets at 9.5% to surpass 5 trillion messages each year. Sms, which is the many used messaging media, will hit 3.2 billion users by 2013.

How Technology Advanced the Way We Write

From the dawn of human development, writing has come a long way. Whether it was etchings on stone, ink on scrolls, or bytes on a word processing program file, humans always discovered innovative methods of interacting. And although the medium used may have been different for each period, the principle of communication which idea of getting a message across stayed the same. Today, however, innovation has assisted us in getting the message across more quickly and precisely than our forefathers did. Simple tools like spelling, autocorrect, and autocomplete, and grammar check have made composing for today's human beings more trouble and mistake complimentary.

Autocomplete Function

The autocomplete function is widespread in lots of applications. Web internet browsers, word processors, integrated advancement environments, and search engines all use some kind of autocompletion performance. The function generally forecasts what the user is intending to type before he/she has finished typing it. It uses the presently typed in characters and calculates the most appropriate word to show.

Establishing code has also gotten faster with the introduction of autocompletion. A coder can simply begin typing and trigger an autocomplete using a keyboard faster way mix. The function either finishes the code or presents the user with a list of possible candidates from which the user can pick. Search engines offer a similar function where the list is ordered based on how often the word or words have been browsed.

Autocorrect Function

This function is comparable to the autocomplete function because it helps the user finish typing a word quicker. The primary difference is it tries to repair mistakes brought on by typographical errors by changing the typed word with the proper one. The word used for replacement is identified by the area of the secrets typed and a dictionary of words matching the series. The iPhone uses this feature to speed up typing text messages. For example, state the user key in "gwkku", autocorrect will see that 'g' is next to 'h,' 'w' is beside e, 'k' is next to 'l,' and 'u' is next to 'o,' therefore deducing that the user was expected to write "hi" rather, and replace the wrong word.

These are simple software application functions that we take for granted every day. They help make our composing lives a lot easier and much faster. On uncommon occasions, nevertheless, they can also backfire on us and make our lives funnier and humiliating. Take the website Autocorrect Fail. When a vehicle appropriate goes wrong, it reveals numerous examples of what may occur.

Understanding Autocorrection

Its primary purpose is as part of the spell checker to correct typical spelling or typing mistakes, conserving time for the user. It is also used to automatically format text or insert unique characters by recognizing specific character usage, saving the user from having to use more laborious functions.

Some writers and organizations choose to regularly change some words with others as part of their editorial policy, with the periodically unforeseen result.

Abuse of text replacement software applications is an essential useful joke in many schools and workplaces. Typically, the prankster will set the victim's data processing software to replace an extremely typical word with a funny absurdity, or an improperly spelled variation of the initial word.

What are some advantages and disadvantages of autocorrect/ autocorrect function?

Advantage: Gives you the word that you're trying to find and/or attempting to spell correctly instantly/immediately on the area

Disadvantage: Gives you the incorrect word and changes a particular word that you're presently using or want to use.

- Coworkers were speaking about their "ejaculation" reports instead of (escalation);.

- A spouse was texting his partner that he "laid" the sitter instead of (paid);.

- A cook was cautioning someone not to touch a bowl of "masturbating" cherries. Instead of

(macerating);.

But What Is Autocorrect, Anyway?

Autocorrect is a software application function commonly found on numerous smart devices and portable web-ready gadgets like the iPod Touch, the efforts to solve common typos on the fly by guessing the word you were trying to write. In theory, Autocorrect's supreme goal is to save time by automating spell checker functions and providing predictions, frequently before you've even ended up typing the whole word.

However, is this function improving our contemporary, super-connected lives?

We move fast, talk quickly, and type fast, and there's no denying Autocorrect can be a big help in these particular scenarios. It often works as the silent hero in the background, making otherwise illegible sentences like "Ehagtimr is ygemewtigg" appear effectively as: "What time is the meeting?".

Autocorrect isn't constantly best. The iPhone, for example, regularly autocorrects "Whitehouse" to "whorehouse" and "homie" to "homoerotic." If you strike "send out" without carefully proofreading, the discussion will surely take an interesting turn and make a jest of you.

So How Does Autocorrect Work?

As it stands today, it's nearly difficult to find information about precisely how the evasive Autocorrect function works. It's a closely safeguarded trade trick among the smartphone companies and software designers, and the majority of them are exceptionally tight-lipped when it concerns discussing it.

The Autocorrect software application checks those letters against a built-in dictionary. If it does not discover an exact match, it thinks what you were attempting to type and uses that word up as a suggestion. Many cell phones also have some sort of "discovering" aspect as well, implying they include brand-new words and terms to the dictionary-based upon the user's behaviors and patterns of usage. As an outcome, after a period of acclimation, no 2 Autocorrect dictionaries may ever be alike.

Smartphones likewise like to insert nonsensical, completely random words that have definitely nothing to do with what you're speaking about. Did somebody state something funny? Beware when replying back with "hahahaha," since it's frequently autocorrected to "Shabaka"-- an Egyptian pharaoh back in 700 BC. The word "funny" typically gets autocorrected to "hoosegow," a slang term for prisoners. And for all my science geeks in the home (cry!), try typing "holy moly" into your phone. On my gadget, I wind up with "holy molybdenum," the chemical aspect with atomic number 42. I'm sure you currently knew that.

Top Twenty-Five Autocorrect Mishaps:

- Word/ phrase you're attempting to write: Hell

  Autocorrected to: He'll.

- Word/ expression you're attempting to write: A sec.

  Autocorrected to: Asexual or sex.

- Word/ expression you're trying to write: Awwwww.

  Autocorrected to: Sewers.

- Word/ expression you're trying to write: Thing.

  Autocorrected to: Thong.

- Word/ phrase you're trying to compose: Bitch.

  Autocorrected to: Birch.

- Word/ expression you're attempting to write: Give me a call

  Autocorrected to: Give me anal.

- Word/ expression you're trying to write: Oooohhh. Autocorrected to: Pooping.

- Word/ phrase you're attempting to write: Grrr. Autocorrected to: Ferret.

- Word/ phrase you're attempting to write: Whenever. Autocorrected to: Wieners.

- Word/ phrase you're trying to compose: Pick me up. Autocorrected to: Oil me up.

- Word/ phrase you're attempting to compose: Keys. Autocorrected to: Jews.

- Word/ phrase you're attempting to write: Shit. Autocorrected to: Shot.

- Word/ phrase you're attempting to compose: Coworkers,

Autocorrected to: Visigoths or Coriander.

- Word/ expression you're attempting to compose: Goooooo.

  Autocorrected to: Hookup.

- Word/ expression you're trying to write: Fucking.
  Autocorrected to: Ducking.

- Word/ expression you're attempting to compose: Hahahaha
  Autocorrected to: Shabaka.

- Word/ phrase you're attempting to write: Homie.
  Autocorrected to: Homoerotic.

- Word/ expression you're trying to compose: Sodium.
  Autocorrected to: Sodomy.

- Word/ phrase you're trying to compose: Mani/Pedi

Autocorrected to: Mani/Penis.

- Word/ expression you're trying to write: Pen.
  Autocorrected to: Penis.

- Word/ phrase you're attempting to compose: Yesyes.
  Autocorrected to: Testes.

- Word/ phrase you're trying to write: Soonish.
  Autocorrected to: Zionism.

- Word/ phrase you're trying to write: Netflix.
- Autocorrected to: Negroid.

- Word/ phrase you're trying to write: Kids.
  Autocorrected to: LSD.
- Word/ phrase you're attempting to compose: Parents.
  Autocorrected to: Parrots.

Another thing that drives individuals "ducking" nuts about the
iPhone and a trend you might have discovered in the above list

is its practically humorous aversion to swearing. It dislikes curse words and does everything in its "ducking" power to avoid you from utilizing them. It even goes so far as to insert an apostrophe in the word HELL (HE'LL), which makes the word take on an entirely different meaning

So now that you understand what Autocorrect is and how it works, you're ready to get to the submissions. Just remember: If you do not desire to end up like one of the poor fellows in this book, type carefully and check your messages or you too might one day find yourself screaming: "FUCK YOU, AUTOCORRECT!".

Turning Off Autocorrect (Not That You' want to!)

Is there a method to turn to Autocorrect off?

Yes, there is! It's an optional function that you can choose to turn off at any time. If you have an iPhone or iPod Touch, tap the Settings icon, then browse to

the General > Keyboard menu. If you have an anDroid, go to Menu > Settings > Language & Keyboard > Device Keyboard, and uncheck Auto-replace. That said, why would you wish to miss out on all the unexpected hilarity! Leave it on! Since we'll be watching, simply keep in mind to proofread before you send something bad!

How to Get Keyword Suggestions in iPhone

The Autocorrect keyboard bar on iPhone is hidden. Fortunately, we can simply make a single change in the code and get the function made it possible for. The autocorrect keyboard bar works in any iOS 5 device, which includes iPhone 4, iPad 2, iPad, iPod Touch 4G, and so on. Things you'll require:

- iBackupBot for Windows/ Mac (whichever OS your system runs).

- An iPhone 4 running iOS 5.

- The latest variation of iTunes for Windows/ Mac.

Let's get that autocorrect keyboard bar made it possible for on your iDevice:

Step One:

Connect your iPhone to your system, and produce a backup of your device through iTunes.

Step Two:

Located and open the backup file through iBackupTool.

Step Three:

Discover this file -> Library/Preferences/com. apple.keyboard.plist.

Step Four:

Add this little piece of code throughout that file:

Conserve the file. (You may get an alert asking you to sign up the software, however you can neglect that as we're going to use it just this as soon as for this procedure. If that message pops up.), Press cancel.

Step Five:

That's it. Backup your iPhone right from iBackupBot with the modified backup file.

When you require to type something, your autocorrect keyboard bar will show up instantly on your iPhone.

About the Autocorrect Keyboard Bar.

The autocorrect keyboard bar is a function that individuals often connect with Android phones. It's unidentified why Apple tried to conceal this and other features deep within the iOS 5; however, it's a great feature if you wish to reduce your time typing and instead get things done quicker.

A word of caution: If you are not that sure about safe modifying (in step four), you can additionally take a backup copy of the backup file you made through iTunes.

Likewise, many individuals walk around saying jailbreak apps allow this feature easily, and you wouldn't have to do anything like including code, etc. But jailbreaking is technically incorrect according to Apple (even though legal according to the law) and can void the guarantee.

So, if all you desire is to make it possible for the autocorrect function, simply use this approach rather than needing to risk a jailbreak.

SECTION TWO

SUPER FUNNY AUTOCORRECT TEXT

FAILS

Silliest Autocorrect Fails

- Bad dialog after the first date.

- **Worst "Happy Birthday" wish to husband**

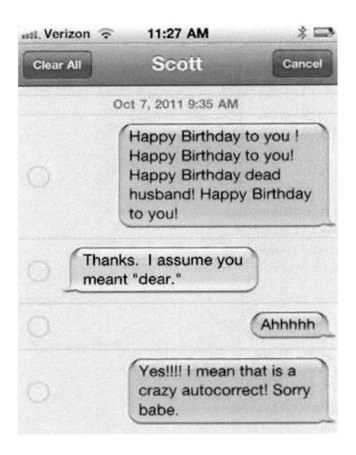

- Friday fun

- **Song about "Hamster Paradise"**

- **I'll be black**

- **Crazy cooking**

Messages (3) Toby Edit

Babe I don't feel like cooking tonight. Can you bring home human beef?

WTF Beth? I'm in a meeting. Human beef? Are you high?

Hunan beef! The place that just opened on 7th ave!!!

I'm laughing so hard I almost puked.

Jesus! I just laughed out loud and could possibly get fired now. :) Order your human beef. I'll pick it up at 6. Love you

autocorrectfail.org Send

- **The date wasn't all right**

- Finding a pencil for the exam

- New color for a room

- About an acquaintance

.ıll AT&T 🛜   **2:39 PM**   ✳ 89% 🔋

< Messages   **Margaret**   Edit

never having them.

Yeah! You know something strange though? In 8th grade my best friend was a girl just like you with redbreasts

RED HAIR!

autocorrectfail.org   Send

- ## What to do when you miss someone

- **Surprise dinner from mom**

- **Break her finger**

- I'm coming over

- It's national coming out day

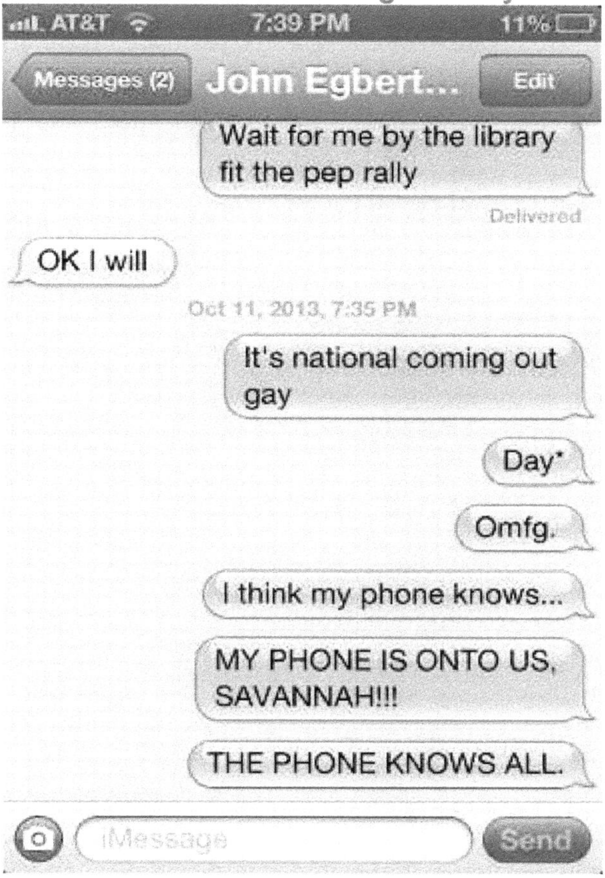

Wait for me by the library fit the pep rally

Delivered

OK I will

Oct 11, 2013, 7:35 PM

It's national coming out gay

Day*

Omfg.

I think my phone knows...

MY PHONE IS ONTO US, SAVANNAH!!!

THE PHONE KNOWS ALL.

iMessage Send

- **You type good**

Messages Tyler <3 Edit

it out. Hasn't really said anything since lol

XD yay

He won't stop plowing me though. It's annoying D<

..lmao wait no. Following.

Feb 1, 2013, 4:50 PM

You type good

Shut up xD

Lol

It was autocorrect D<

Mhm. Sure.

Text Message Send

46

- Open your pool

- **I'll bring a blanket**

I'll bring a blanket and we'll make it a cut dick date :)

Hahahahah omg dock*

> Hahahahahha

😂 😂 😂

- **I am Gollum**

I am not mom
I am golly
You are precious she's
she's southbound

> southbound?

Holy typos/autocorrect,
batman

Holy typos/autocorrect,
batman

> What did you mean?

> ??

I am gollum
You are
precioussssssssssssss
sssss

48

- **To smoke or not to smoke**

Messages   **Kailie**   Contact

K

To smoke or not to smoke
that is the weed question

To be or not to be that is
the real question

> My dads on this phone.

Read 6:44 PM

I

- **Wanna you go babdos?**

Messages **Esme** 🖤🖤   Details

I'll be round for 6:15 xxx

> Ok you wanna go
> babdos?

> Babdos

> Babdos

What

> Ducking nandos

Lol

> Fucking nandos

Delivered

Yes!!!!!!!

😂😂😂😂😂

49

- ## I rest all weekend

Sprints 🏃‍🏃‍

We will take it easy tomorrow and just work on form

> No we won't lol

> I rest all wknd, may as well milk myself tmrw

> Hahaha kill no milking

Read 7:40 AM

😂😂😂😂😂😂

That was funny

- ## I try not

← ★ Arasnady or Tsirkmaharg ⋮

> I try not to play with fire or poke beats

pride .... my face hurts

> Bears

lions???

Some people drop the beat, Dan pokes it

> It's called dub-skip

Dan - the white bread dubskip

DVD and bluray

> My initials are already DJ

DJ Bro. dubskip pioneer

50

- ## You are vehicular

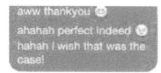

You are vehicular!!

Beautiful'

- ## I'm going to get drunk

Plus you're going to be my uber the entire time I'm in town and I'm going to get drunk and sleep on my dads body for a week.

WHAT?

Did you proofread that last sentence there

Or are you just into that sort of thing haha?

Omgggggggg

I'm crying

Boattttttt

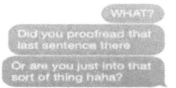

Hahahaha

51

Common Comic Text Fails

I'm all in bed and sleepy

I love Hulu

That was supposed to say "you" and not Hulu

I only like Hulu as a friend

Mom

We can look at them tomorrow or tuesday when we go heterosexual the food for thanksgiving

When we go heterosexual?

Nov 20, 2011 8:15 PM

I hate this phone , when we get the food for thanksgiving

Lol

Nov 20, 2011 11:05 PM

Do you want to do this at your house? we won't have to be so quite.

Mackenzie

Ugg I have had the worst day ever

Aw I'm so sorry hon

I just want you to fist me when I get home and make me forget all about it.

(•).(•)
O

HAHAHAH KISS ME!!! Lol. Well at least I'm laughing now.

LILY Cell

Feb 17, 2011 1:58 PM

I look forward to the day when I'm not blowing minors every day.

Uhhhhh...

Blowing minors?

My nose!!!! Omg! Lmao!

I'm sick :(

Sarah M

can we set up a phone call for thisafternoon?

Today isn't good. I'll be in and out of cunt all day. Tomorrow will be better.

Autocorrect. I meant court. I'm sincerely sorry.

Well this is awkward. I'll be in touch tomorrow then. Thank you.

55

Mom

meh. still feel like crap :(

have u tried taking some dicks?

OMG VICKS!!! HAVE YOU TAKEN SOME VICKS!!!!

omg mom!!

im am LMFAO-ing rite now ^^

yea yea just dont tell your father about this.

Maria

It's too damn cold outside!

Ugh. I know! I'm just curling up with a cup of Nazi ball soup.

You did not just say that.

gah! Matzo ball soup. You know I'm Jewish right?

Just don't spill any Nazi balls on you hahaha

58

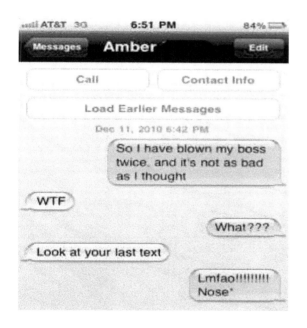

59

Nov 28, 2010 10:15

Well there's a few really good scotch bars around so gimmie anal when you want to go again.

Ummmmm are you sure? I can just text you; less intrusive.

Why would anything auto correct to anal?? *a call!

No anal, no scotch. Them's the rules. :)

Damn phone

Sabrina

Besssssstttttt friendddddddd

Yeeeeeessss my looooooove!

Soooooooo.... Can u wake me up in the meningitis

Wtffffffff

Wtf?!?!?

Meningitis?????

Omg I'm LAUGHING MY ASS OOOOOFFFFF!!!!

Lmfaoooooooo

60

The only plans I have that day are getting new penis

Omg! Pants!

Hahahahahahaha ok

I don't think my forever21 giftcard will work for that

Hahaha I don't wanna get penis with you but I'm down for hp!

are you hungry?

Starving

I thought you might be. There's a huge surprise waiting for you in the kitchen. It's your favorite. Love Mom.

I hope it's your shaved pussy

Omg

Please don't read that last text it was the worst autocorrect of my life

I meant porkkkkk shaved pork I'm so sorry Ma

Mom?

hey dude can you come over later to help fix my cock?

its making weird sounds and every once in a while it'll stop randomly and i cant get it to turn back on with out attacking it

sounds like a personal problem there man. call a doctor?

ah F*CK! i meant CLOCK help fix my CLOCK

oh.. well i just forwarded this whole convo to your girlfriend you got some explaining to do

•• Fido 🤖   9:00 PM   42% 💬

< Messages   **Blair**   Contact

it's OK, I'm not really sure what you said exactly.. :-)

Send

Ewwq

Ewww LIES

I SHIT IN MY DICKYARD

trololol.

then my neighbours are like "wtf are you doing?!" and i'm like "i'm shitting."

LOLOLOLOLOL >:)

'backyard

lol my stupid thumbs

I SHIT IN MY VAGINAYARD.

Text Message   Send

I have gained 10 foreskin pounds since I stopped smoking!!!!

LMAO!!! Freaking!!!! OMG

Jan 20, 2012 10:13 AM

OMG!!! I think that I would just start smoking again. Who really need be be carrying around 10 extra pounds of FORESKIN. Plus it could easily start to smell really bad!

Jan 20, 2012 10:34 AM

I am not the one carrying around 10lbs of foreskin!!!

Send

64

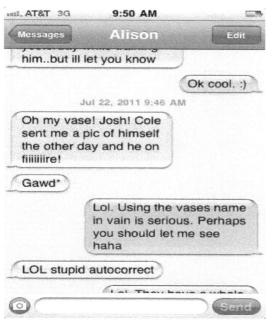

Alison

him..but ill let you know

Ok cool. :)

Jul 22, 2011 9:46 AM

Oh my vase! Josh! Cole sent me a pic of himself the other day and he on fiiiiiire!

Gawd*

Lol. Using the vases name in vain is serious. Perhaps you should let me see haha

LOL stupid autocorrect

Eion

Call | Contact Info

Apr 24, 2011 12:27 PM

Hey u, just seeing how ur doing. Lol

I'm eating a kitten and a guitar today!! :D

What? Lol

Lmao I meant getting a kitten and a guitar!!! Stupid auto correct.

66

How was your night?

I almost got murdered by that anal and then went to bed.

ANIMAL*****

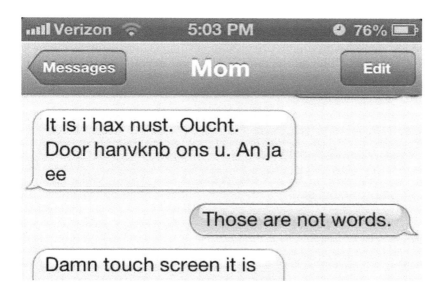

It is i hax nust. Oucht. Door hanvknb ons u. An ja ee

Those are not words.

Damn touch screen it is

Great news - Grandma is homosexual!

Okay?

Homo hot lips

Hot tulips

I am getting fisted now

Frustrated

Grandma is h o m e

from h o s p i t a l

Hahaha homo hot lips!!??

Shut up lol

HAHAHAH

Jun 20, 2013, 4:29 PM

I just ripped a huge hole in my shit :(

Shaft*

Shin*

Saint*

Damage! Start!

....

Delivered

Wtf man. S H I R T.

69

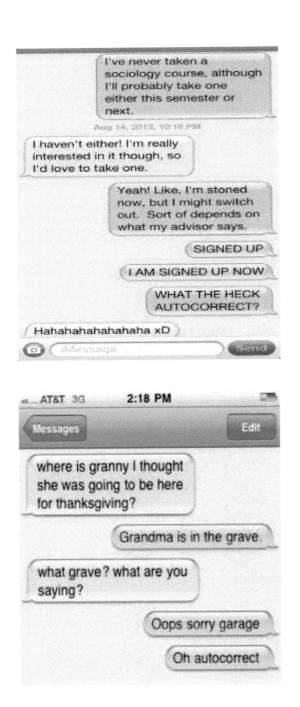

I've never taken a sociology course, although I'll probably take one either this semester or next.

Aug 14, 2013, 10:18 PM

I haven't either! I'm really interested in it though, so I'd love to take one.

Yeah! Like, I'm stoned now, but I might switch out. Sort of depends on what my advisor says.

SIGNED UP

I AM SIGNED UP NOW

WHAT THE HECK AUTOCORRECT?

Hahahahahahahaha xD

iMessage   Send

AT&T 3G   2:18 PM

Messages   Edit

where is granny I thought she was going to be here for thanksgiving?

Grandma is in the grave.

what grave? what are you saying?

Oops sorry garage

Oh autocorrect

70

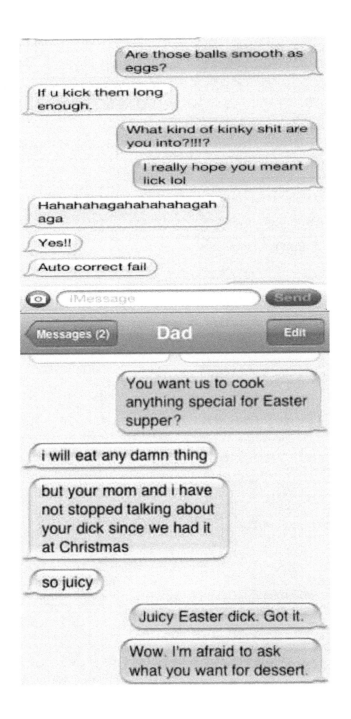

Are those balls smooth as eggs?

If u kick them long enough.

What kind of kinky shit are you into?!!!?

I really hope you meant lick lol

Hahahahagahahahahagah aga

Yes!!

Auto correct fail

iMessage   Send

Messages (2)   Dad   Edit

You want us to cook anything special for Easter supper?

i will eat any damn thing

but your mom and i have not stopped talking about your dick since we had it at Christmas

so juicy

Juicy Easter dick. Got it.

Wow. I'm afraid to ask what you want for dessert.

FriendsChats GetAutocorrected

Creepy Birthday

Dogsitting

What's That Smell?

Christmas Gifts

Fitness Regime

Hey, whatever works

Pics or It Didn't Happen!

Christmas Music

Concert

Stage an Intervention

Time of the Month

Very
Presidential

Running Errands

Somebody Call DCS!

Toilets

Accidental
Insult

Paint Color

Great Seats

The Old Adage

Magical School

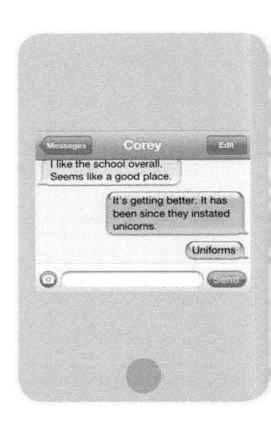

Housekeeping

Clothing
Options

What's That Smell?

Insomnia

Get Well Soon

All in the Family

Pampering

Great Story, Bro

New Baby

The Wizard

Empty-Handed

Adopting a Dog

House Hunting

Sounds
Painful

Send Help!

Congratulations

Dropping Hints

Dad's Christmas Present

Happy for you

Bah, Humbug!

Lather, Rinse, Repeat

Sounds Like a Great Party

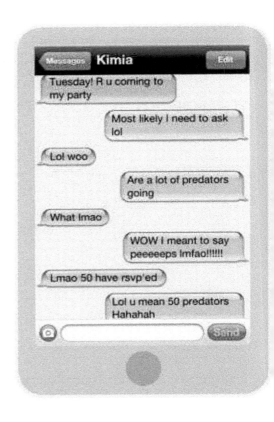

On the Road Again

Decorations

Day Off

Moving
Day

Road Rage

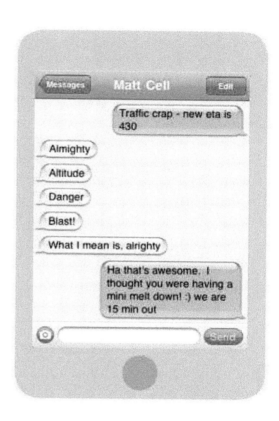

Memorable Pics of Dad

Shhh...

Movie
Snacks

Ribbit,
Ribbit

Samantha's Boyfriend

Whoops

Thanks, I Think

Tragic
Christmas

Get in the
Zone

Higher
Learning

I'll meet you @ 6:00? I'm taking a new fart class. Be done by 5:45.

What type of things do you do in these "FART" classes? Not sure I want to meet up after youve been there for hours! LMAO.

Oh. My. God. ART CLASS. Renaissance Fine Art. No flatulence. I hope. See you at 6?

Get Some
Sleep

Out with the Boys

How
Festive

New Puppy

Bikes from Santa

Autocorrect On Timing

Lawyer
Fail

Mondays Are Rough

Rise and Shine

That's a Bad Day

Lunch

Office
Party

Another Cubicle

Work
Retreat

Anger Management

Head in the Workplace

Important Meeting

Tough Commute

Is That Harassment?

Before the Meeting

Long Lunch

Helping Hand

Considerate Coworkers

Bills

Office Supply Cabinet

Calling Out

Favors

New
Position

Extra
Hours

Time for a Raise

Lost
Promotion

Stimulating Job

Working from Home

Day at Work

Hooking Up the New Monitor

Sounds
Dangerous

Tech Support

Day Off

Slow Day

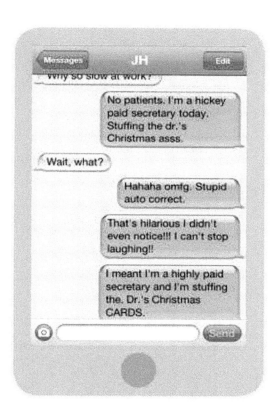

Workin' Day and Night

The Herb?

Early Morning Issues

Servers
Down

AwkwardTextswithMom & Dad

The Big "D"

Mom's Office Fight

Ducks and Jackets

Scaring
Mom

Hot for teacher

Way TMI for Dad

Girls' Night

Happy Birthday, Mom

Messages from Beyond

Shopping for Dad

Thanks, Mum!

Technology

Dinner
Options

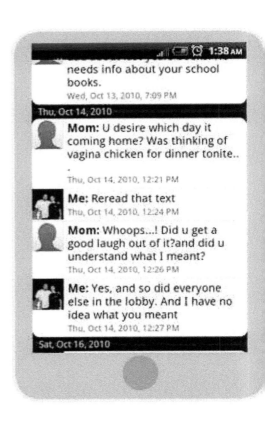

We've All Been There

Where's Dad?

Our Little Secret

Chores

Accidental Insult

Finals Week

Chew on This

Robot
Invasion

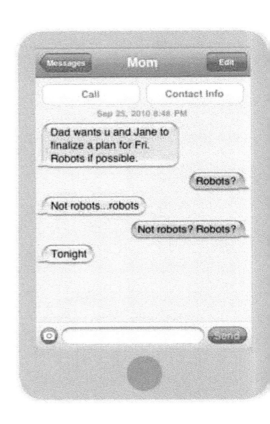

Under the Weather

Thanksgiving Work

Day at the Salon

Babysitter Needed

Is Mom Okay?

Arts & Crafts

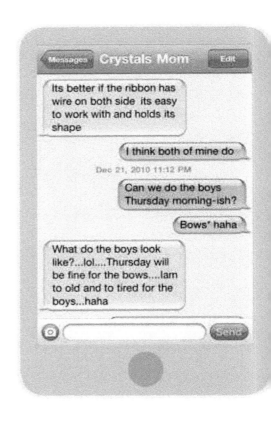

Time Off

Waiting for Mom

Return to
Sender

Ready,
Freddie

Dad's Wish List

Duck
Hunting

Checking In

Gee,
Thanks

Very Dirty Harry

A Simple
Request

House
Sitting

Job
Options

Ho-Ho-Horrible

Dinner
Plans

In for a Visit

When Dads Shop...

Fourth of July

Jeez, Mom!

CongratDad

Charm

Yellow
Pages

Christmas
Presents

When Couples TextGone Wrong

Advice Don't Mix

Autocorrected Break-up

Bad Girl

Arguing OverText

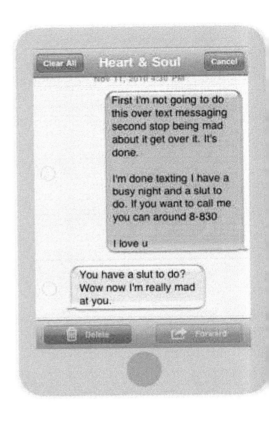

Sexting Gone Wrong

Terms of Endearment

Crybaby

A Night Apart

The Babysitter

Love

Secret's Out

Date Night

A Night In

Hidden Desires

Need to GetWorried?

The Crush

Drunk Dialing

The Mall & More

Bedtime Wishes

Grocery Shopping

Measure of Time

Backhanded Compliment

Common Cold

Bad Kissers

Surprise!

Nighty
Night

So
Romantic

Living
Together

I Love You

The New Guy

AutocorrectedFood & BeverageText

Bowl!

Special
Dinner

Anniversary Meal

Bomb
Squad

Trader
Joe's

Mom

Rosemary and Rhyme

Dinner at the Office

Eating Out

Yum-O

Snack Time!

Italian
Food

Romantic
Dinner

Swine

No Means No,

Shop Order

Lunch
Invite

In
Treatment

Empty Fridge

Ahoy,
Matey

Other Plans

Edible
Filipinos

Snap, Crackle, WTF?

General
Tso

Shopping
List

New Food Group

Snack Time

Mom's Hungry

Dinner for One

Deadly
Dinner

How to Cook
Lentils

No Soup for you

If You Say So

Rain Check

Grandpa Soul for Lunch

Sweeping the Nation

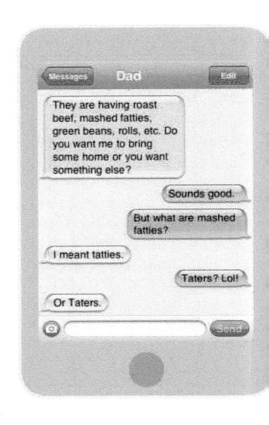

Failed Text Predicting The Mind

WeekendCook out

Intriguing Offer

Weekend Plans

Big Boned

Evening Entertainment

Boob Tube

Game
Night

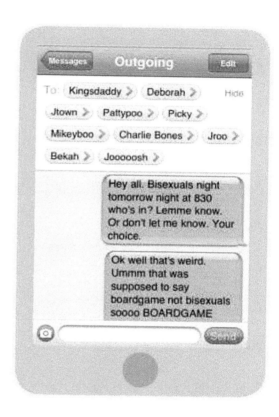

Asking a Favor

Such a Hassle

Dirty Mind

Awkward

New Airport Wing

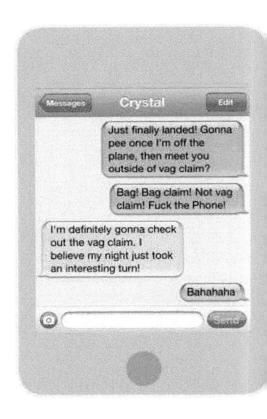

Planning the Evening

Quick Stop

Sounds Cold

Thirst

Spring
Break

ID

OWN Network

Bromance

Wasting the Day

So Much Confusion

Dinner at 5

Rachael's Party

Matthew's Bae

Crash and Burn

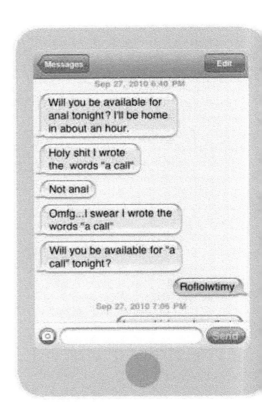

Beware of Santa

Two Hours

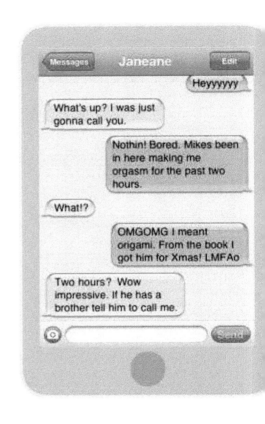

Neighborhood

PhotoShoot

The Holidays

Sore Throat

Interesting Events

Open
Schedule

Movie
Night

Can You Sense It?

Thanks for Sharing

Take
YourTime

Reminders

Dangers of Kickboxing

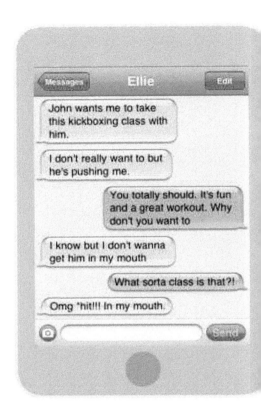

TotallyRandom
AutocorrectIncident

Shabaka!

Dinosaur Infection

Dancing
Queen

Baby

Sounds
Serious

Bring Your Bunsen Burner

Greeting
Fail

What!

Zionism

Coach Rockne

Messages (2) | Joey | Edit

Thank you

You're Rockne!

.........are you kidding me phone.

Apparently you are a US football coach that was born in norway.

Did I lead my team to any victories?

You are regarded as one of the greatest coaches in college football history

Periodic Table of WTF

Mom's Present

Fuzzy
Flowers

this is gonna be all you hear about in nerdland when the USA version drops. The books, of course, are already HUGE beardtongues.

what in the fuck?

HOW IN THE SHIT DID "BESTSELLERS" GET AUTOCORRECTED TO "BEARDTONGUES"?

I do not know and am horrified.

BADONKADONK!

French
Armchairs

Seriously, Phone?

Don't Be a Joe Bagel

Sounds Kinda Far

Birds

Pizza Toppings

Yellow Flowering Plants

Noisy &
Outspoken

Autobiography

Cold Outside

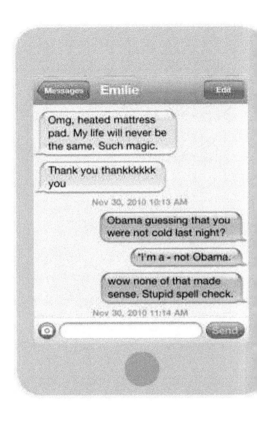

Cool
Feature

The text messages shown read:

Kelsey

There's an inside pocket on this peacock!!! Awesomeee

Peacoat

Not the bird

Traffic
Update

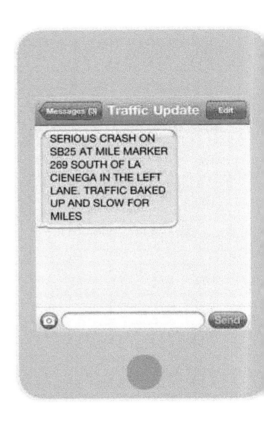

Coffee Run

Head Coverings

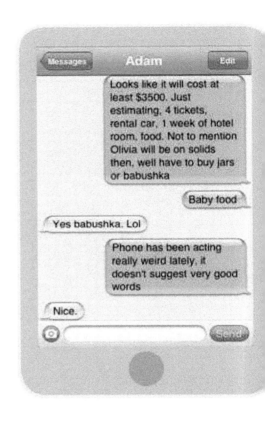

Messages   Adam   Edit

Looks like it will cost at least $3500. Just estimating, 4 tickets, rental car, 1 week of hotel room, food. Not to mention Olivia will be on solids then, well have to buy jars or babushka

Baby food

Yes babushka. Lol

Phone has been acting really weird lately, it doesn't suggest very good words

Nice.

Yesssssssssss!

Firefighter

"Is That a Word?!"

Out of Nowhere

New Year's Eve

Sisterly
Bonding

Lightning Source UK Ltd.
Milton Keynes UK
UKHW030643140121
377037UK00010B/981